In My Feelings Series

V O L U M E II

OTHER BOOKS BY ROBERT M. DRAKE

Spaceship (2012)
The Great Artist (2012)
Science (2013)
Beautiful Chaos (2014)
Beautiful Chaos 2 (2014)
Black Butterfly (2015)
A Brilliant Madness (2015)
Beautiful and Damned (2016)
Broken Flowers (2016)
Gravity: A Novel (2017)
Star Theory (2017)
Chaos Theory (2017)
Light Theory (2017)
Moon Theory (2017)
Dead Pop Art (2017)
Chasing The Gloom: A Novel (2017)
Moon Matrix (2018)
Seeds of Wrath (2018)
Dawn of Mayhem (2018)
The King is Dead (2018)
What I Feel When I Don't Want To Feel (2019)
What I Say To Myself When I Need To Calm The Fuck Down (2019)
What I Say When I'm Not Saying A Damn Thing (2019)
What I Mean When I Say Miss You, Love You & Fuck You (2019)
What I Say To Myself When I Need To Walk Away, Let Go And Fucking Move On (2019)
What I Really Mean When I Say Good-bye, Don't Go And Leave Me The Fuck Alone (2019)
The Advice I Give Others But Fail To Practice My Damn Self (2019)
The Things I Feel In My Fucking Soul And The Things That Took Years To Understand (2019)

For Excerpts and Updates please follow:

Instagram.com/rmdrk
Facebook.com/rmdrk
Twitter.com/rmdrk

ISBN: 978-1-7326901-4-1

Book Cover: Robert M. Drake

For The Ones Who Feel Like They've Lost
Everything

CONTENTS

WHAT I SAY TO MYSELF WHEN I NEED TO WALK AWAY, LET GO AND FUCKING MOVE ON

ROBERT M. DRAKE

WHAT WE WANT

All of my life
I've been told

to wait.

To be patient.

To just
let things happen

on their own.

All of my life
I've been led

to believe,
that if

it's meant
for me

then I shouldn't
have to

worry
about anything.

That

if it's written...
it will occur.

That

it will come
to me.

And in all my years,
I've been waiting...

in all my years,
I've let

so many things
pass me by.

I've lost too much
and I've gained...

too little.

I've given my soul
and I've received

barely anything
back

in return.

So I don't

want to believe
that if it's meant

to happen,
then

I should just
let things be

on their own.

Let things
come to me

at their own
pace.

No.
fuck that.

If I have a dream
I want to work on it.

I want to
believe in it.

Envision it
for my own.

I want to build
on it.

Day by day.
Hour by hour.

Until one day,
I wake up,

look back
and see

all the progress
I've made.

I want to believe
in myself

and not just
destiny.

I want to trust
what I'm capable of.

Trust
what I know

can be done.

And it's the same thing
with you.

I don't want to
wait around anymore.

I don't want to
watch you slip

through my hands.

I want to work on *us*.

Day by day.
Hour by hour.

I want to feed
your heart

and water
your soul.

I want to let
things be

but only because
we let it be.

Because

we want it
to be.

Let me be your sun.
Your moon.

Your planet.

Let me be
the lover you need.

Let me follow you.
Grow with you.

Heal with you.

To fill the cracks
and the void.

Let me love you
and let me do it now...

unconditionally
and without

regret.

I don't want to waste
my time

waiting around for you
to be mine.

I don't want to sit around
and wonder.

Let us sit
on the sun

with all reason,
and let us create

a place

where all the things
we want to happen...

happen

but only
because we want them

to
and only

because we put the effort
in all the things

we want
to stay.

FEEL ME NOW

Feel me.

I have more soul
than you think.

More pain.
More laughter.

More tears.
More love.

Feel me.

From the moment
you met me,

to the moment
we said good-bye.

I have always
had more.

I have always
felt more...

but I have also,
shared less.

Said less
and the moment

you met me,
I loved you.

I had it
in for you.

For us.

For what
we could have been.

But instead,
I let myself drown.

I let myself
drift away.

I let myself
hurt you,

the only person
I could trust.

Goddamn
it's a fucking shame.

It really is.
And I still

don't understand
why I did

what I did
to you.

I still don't understand
why I push

people away.

Why I have this
tendency

to distance myself
from the people

I love
or why

I have this
terrible habit

to detach myself
from anything

and anyone
who gets too close.

Maybe I'm afraid
of loss.

Maybe I'm afraid
of getting hurt first.

Of being broken
by someone

I thought
who'd always be there

for me.

It's ironic,
I know.

I break the people
I love.

I leave the people
whom I want

to stay.

Just feel me
on this one.

Just try to understand.

It's me.
It's not you.

It's really me.

The thing is,
I don't know what

to do
with all of this love

I have trapped
within me.

And I don't know
how

to let it out
properly…

but it does
have a hold of me.

And I wish
I could have shared it

with you.

But instead,
I let you go

without reason
and let you go...

with regret
and I'm sorry

for that.

Someway,
somehow,

for me,

my story
always ends

with being alone…
but that is something

I have to live
with on my own.

It is my own burden.

My own curse.

CAN BE DONE

And yes,
it might be true.

You can't heal
another human.

You can't rid them
of their demons

or of their past.

But you could
sit with them

while they're breaking
apart.

You could
keep them

a little company
when they feel

most alone.

You could take the time
to listen to them.

To try to put yourself
in their shoes

and understand.

Yes,
of course,

it is true.

I can't make you
happy.

I can't wash away
what's in your heart.

What's been ticking
within your mind.

What's been
eating you alive.

No.

But I could
be there for you.

I could
love you

and I could

go through the fire
with you.

So you don't
have to walk alone.

You don't
have to think

no one
is out there

anymore.

You don't have to
pretend

or try
to be

someone else
because it hurts.

No.

You don't have to.

Not anymore
and it doesn't have to be

like this

either.

So yes,
I can't heal you.

I can't promise you
infinite laughter

and I can't
promise you

the stars.

But hell,
I can sure

fucking try.

I can sure
fucking put my heart in—all

of it, too.

And I can
be real with you.

And I can
make sure

every moment counts.
That's all I have.

That's all I feel
in my heart.

I'll save you
no matter what,

even if they say
it can't

be done.

I'll be there.
Always.

PEOPLE LIKE US

You have to
constantly be

reminded
of your worth.

Of what
you're capable of

and of what
you deserve.

You have to
constantly be surrounded

by good things.

By good food.
By good music.

By good life
and good company.

You have to constantly
be indulge

in these things
or at least

try to be.

Because
there are too many
things

that kill the soul
out here.

Too much hate.
Too much detachment.

Too much separation
and bigotry.

With all these things
being shoved

down our throats
you need

something
to bring you back

toward the light
or someone

to guide you back
toward the shore.

So this is why

I want to
help you

find what inspires you
again.

What brings you back
to where

you belong.

And I know
nothing is ever

promised.

And I know
nothing lasts

forever.

But there is more
beyond today.

More
beyond what we could

imagine.

More inspiration
to be found.

More love
to be dug

out from the depths
of our souls.

More unity.
More friendship.

More genius.

More things
to save humanity.

More peace.

Yes.

There is always
more fucking peace

to be found.

We have so many
useless things

around us
that are meant

to destroy
what matters most.

Useless things
that are meant

to devour
what brings

people like us
together.

So there you have it.

This is why
I am always reminding you

to love yourself
a little harder.

To put yourself
first

sometimes—that
it's okay

to say no
if you don't believe in it.

This is why
I always encourage

your happiness.

Encourage
what makes you

keep going.

We have so much
fucking darkness

all around us,
so there's no need

for us
to live

these blind lives,
following

these blind leaders.

Doing
and thinking

how they want us
to think.

You have me
and I have you...

and we need each other.

More people like us,

you know?

The world is cold.
The depths of the oceans
remain untouched.

And somewhere
in-between

there's us.

Two people
searching for more.

Two people
who constantly

have to remind themselves
that they

deserve more.

We are searching
for liberation

from everything
we've been told.

Break free.

IT IS EASY

It's easy to be cruel
but it takes guts

to be kind.
To swallow our pride.

To admit
when you're wrong.

It takes strength
to make things work.

Perseverance
to make things last.

And it takes courage
to let someone know

how you feel.

So you're not weak
and being good to people

doesn't make you crazy.

You're not fragile
for recognizing your flaws.

And you're definitely not

naive

for letting people know
what's in your heart—for believing

what's in it
and for giving it

to those who need it
most.

So yes,
it's easy to hate—to
be spread lies—to

put others down
but that's not who you are.

You're beautiful, baby.

You're kind
and giving
and loving at the same time...

and that's a gift
more than a curse.

So take it in.

Embrace it.

Don't let the negativity
change a goddamn thing.

You are who you are

and

I wouldn't trade that
for the world.

BACK TO THIS ON TO THIS

Now let's get back to this.

Let's get down to it.
To what it could mean.

To what it says
about us

and what it represents.

Are we that broken?
Are we that hurt—so much

that we can't let go?
Are we that fucked up?

So much
that we are convinced
that this is normal?

I love you
but you're no good to me

and I don't know
what to do,

there seems to be
no end to this.

No final chapter, you know?

We make up.
We break up.

And the venom from our love
weakens our judgment.

Weakens our ability
to make rational decisions,

and every time
we get back together again…

it seems
as if we don't care...

but care enough
to not let go.

I think of us,
I think of what would be

the end of us
and if it will ever come...

and if we'll be ready
for it:

to let go
and start over

as new people
with other people, too.

I think of our lives,
what it was before us.

If we were happy
or if we were the same way

but with other people.

I think about us, you know?

If it's me
that causes this

or if it's you
and maybe

I'm just another sucker
you take advantage of.

Another sucker
you have tangled

on the tips of your fingers.

Or maybe it's the other way around.

Because I'm a real bastard
sometimes, you know?

A real son of a bitch.

Because I like to pull your strings.

I like to push you back
every time you push me

a little harder toward the edge.

But I love you,
nonetheless, I think I do,

I feel it.

But I also hate you.

I can't stand you
sometimes, you know?

And it's black
and white with us.

We either in love
sharing a dinner

or fighting
spending our nights alone,
crying,

wondering who will be the first
to admit defeat.

The first
to give in,

cave in, you know?

It's a war with us sometimes
and it's unfortunate.

Because yes,
maybe we both could be happy
with other people.

Maybe we could be
in love with other people, too.

But here we are
miserable sometimes,

vicious and terribly
in love with both our sides.

With both the light
and the darkness.

With both the paradise
and the horrors we bring.

Our walls are shaken.
Our bones are brittle.

Our minds are exhausted.

Our doors are blown
to pieces

and our hearts
belong to one another…

no matter how difficult
things get.

If that's not love
then I don't know what it is

and I wouldn't want to know
either way.

REGRETS (LONG VERSION)

I gave up
on her.

I had to.

I couldn't ingest
why.

I think
I didn't even care.

I started drinking
the night before.

Not because
I was sad

over what
had happened

but because
I felt

like I had nothing
else to do.

Nothing else
to live for.

After going through
so much disappointment.

I felt
like it was

the next thing
to do.

The next chapter.

The next road
to walk through.

Maybe it was destiny
or maybe

the stars lined up
for me

and a miracle
happened.

But after
my eleventh beer

I began to write.

Something
inside of me
just flowed.

Of course,
it was far

from the social
paradigms.

I didn't want
to sound

too smart.

I didn't want
to sound

too dumb.

I just wanted
to create.

Nothing too serious
or humorous.

I just wanted
to create something real.

Something
I was feeling

from within
my bones.

One word
after another.

Until I was
completely finished.

Soon after,
I began to weep

and I wasn't even sure
why.

Maybe I felt
unlucky.

Maybe I felt
more lost

than before.

More intoxicated
than before.

More in love
than before.

I didn't have
a choice.

I had to
let her go.

I didn't want
to be labeled.

I didn't want
to be the bad guy.

I'm a sucker,
you know?

I love too much
but I show it

too little.

The God's
made me this way.

Made me
with more flaws

than strengths.

With more doubts
than truths.

With more questions
than answers.

I gave up on her,
and maybe

it was the wrong thing
to do

or the right thing
to do,

blindly.

I felt alone that night—more
alone than ever.

Like an outsider
but also

very free.

I gave up
I had to.

It was the last thing
I did.

The first moment
I wrote

and wrote
and wrote.

Death I'm ready for.

The words

are forever
and the woman

I once loved
is gone.

She is lost in a world
full of assholes

and I'd like
to believe

that every night
she thinks of me

just as much
as I think

about her.

There is always something
or someone

you regret
letting go.

I want to forget—to
go back

to how my life was

before *you.*
Before her.

And I know
it sounds harsh,

but hear me out.

Let me try to be honest
with you here.

Sometimes
I feel like

I want to leave.

Like I want
to let go.

Like I want
to run away

as far
as my legs

can take me
but you know me
to well.

You know
that if I wander away

that eventually,
I'll find my way back

to you.

You know
that I sometimes say things

out of anger,
out of pain

but you also know
that I don't mean them.

You also know
that I regret

the way I carelessly am
with you.

It's hard
keeping my cool.

It's just,
I care so fucking much

about your happiness
that sometimes

I feel
like I'm not

the right person
for you.

Sometimes
I feel

like you can do better.

Like you deserve
better.

I care so fucking much
that sometimes

I can't control
what it is

I feel.

And that's why
sometimes

I want to get away.

Because I feel
like I'm not enough.

Because I feel
no matter how hard

I try

to make things work.

I keep drifting
our relationship

more toward
the darkness.

More toward
oblivion.

But can you blame me?

This is
all I know.

This is
how I've grown.

I don't know
any better.

My hands break things.

They're too hard
to hold your hands

softly.

Too clumsy
and too dumb

to keep your heart
steady.

I am trying,
God knows

I am
but it is in

my nature
to hurt the people

I love.

To push them away.
I've done it before.

Like I said,
I can't help it

no matter how hard
I try.

I'm sorry,
kid.

I've got to go
this time.

I wouldn't be able
to live with myself

if I made you
cry again.

I won't stand for it.

And this might be
a grave mistake

but I must go.

Please know,
that I do

love you deeply
and I will miss you

and I will think of you
when I feel

most alone.

I'll never forget you.

I just want
you to be happy

even if
it's not

with me.

NEED THEM

The people
who understand you

and the people
who are there for you...

also get tired—also
have bad days.

They also
have their own

problems
and they also

feel the way
you feel

sometimes.

So please
be gentle with them.

Be kind with them.

They're just as soft
as you are

and
they need you

just as much
as you need them.

The world
is not the same

without them.

So we
must always show
them

that we, too,
care.

SACRIFICE

Sacrifice
is love sometimes.

Swallowing your pride
and your ego

is sometimes love.

It's not pretty
to try

to make things
work

and who ever said
it was...

is a fucking asshole.

You want
to find love?

You want
to find peace

in love?

Then you must

let go
a piece of yourself.

You must
find a balance

between who you are
and who

you want to be.

You have to sacrifice
something.

That's how
it is sometimes.

No one
is perfect.

But by understanding
and respecting

one another,
then by all means,

something special
could be achieved.

That is all
we want

ultimately.

Understanding,
unconditional love

but not many of us
are willing

to accept
the flaws.

To accept
the horrors

of it all.

Most of us
only want

the pretty things.

Most of us
only want

what we've been told
to find.

To find
the "perfect one."

This I say

to you,

that...
that

is a goddamn lie
told by these

corporations
that want to sell you

the idea

that the "perfect love" exist.

This I say,
to my friends,

to my family,
to my readers

across the goddamn globe
and I take this

to the grave.

So please
engrave it

on my tombstone.

Do not fall
for that illusion.

Do not believe
that the perfect love

is out there.

You will search
and search and search

and never find it.

You will come up
short

every time.

Find someone
who completes you.

Who makes you
feel alive.

Who gives you
fire.

Who allows you
to be yourself,

flaws and all.

Find someone
who admires your dreams.

Who'll support them,
who'll do you

more good
than harm.

Find someone,
anyone... it's okay

to be alone
sometimes

but it is sad
to feel

completely alone.

Everyone needs someone
to lean on.

Someone
to talk to

without feeling judged.

Without feeling
some kind of way

after,
you know?

Find someone
who contradicts themselves

sometimes.

Find someone
who makes peace

with their demons
and yours.

Find someone
who's been through things.

Who been defeated
and understands

what it's like
to be under pressure.

Under stress
and fear

and has
moved forward

from them.

Find someone
who's capable

of saving themselves.

And someone
who has the heart

to save others—to
try to save others

even if they know
they can't.

The list can go on.

But the bottom line is,
to just find someone

who makes you
happy.

All else
means nothing.

All else
is meant

to take so much
out of you

but also
give so much

less
in return.

A CHANCE

I never got
the chance

to meet you.

I never got
the chance

to show you
how much

I care.

And all of that
is sad,

but what's worse
is...

how you never got
the chance

to see
how much of you

I have.

How much

of you
I resemble.

You never got
the chance

to see
what has

become of me.

And that's
what hurts

the most.

NO MATTER WHAT

My entire life
has been dedicated

to you.

It has been
dedicated

to your
well-being—for

ours.

Both mental
and physical.

I don't want
to hurt you

and I know
you don't want

to hurt me
either.

You see,
I want us

to be happy.

I want us
to succeed.

I want us
to only sacrifice

the parts
of ourselves

we no longer
need.

To let go
of the past

and move forward.

I want us
to be real

with one another.

To not let
our egos

stop us
from feeling the things

we want to feel.

From sharing the things
we want to share.

And from being open
with one another

without any
kind of regret

or any doubt.

I know
this might sound

naive
but I believe

it can be done,
that is,

if we both try
hard enough—if

we want it
bad enough.

If we're both
willing

to unlearn
everything

we've learned
about love

and start over.

The thing is,
we can create

our own laws,
our own order.

We don't need the chaos
to create

something beautiful.

We don't need
the pain

to appreciate
the goodness we deserve.

We don't need
to follow

what we've experience
before—to

make sure
things fall into place

as they should.

And we don't need
guidance

to make our own path.

What we need
is each other.

And I don't just mean
you
and me

but everything
we need

to survive.

*All of our beliefs
and goals.*

All of our dreams
and nightmares.

All of our failures
and fears.

Our hopes
and memories.

Because I want you
for you

and I'll dedicate
my entire life

rehearsing

this over
and over.

Until the moon collapses
into the ocean

and the sun vanishes
before our eyes.

I love you.
I love you.
I love you.

So please,

let these be
the words

that fill your heart
when you feel empty.

Let these be
the words

that accompany you
when you feel

most alone.

I love you,

I will always
feel this

with you
and I'll dedicate my entire

life
proving that to you.

No matter what.

RISE AGAIN

You will fall.

You will break.

You will hurt
and you will cry

but you will
also

learn to rise
again.

SOMETHING LIKE THAT

If they want
to be with you,

they'll show you.

And if they care,
they'll show it

carefully.

They'll make sure
to let you know

how they feel.

And they won't
leave you

stranded
in a pool

made of broken dreams
and they definitely

won't make you
question them

neither.

It's something
you'll just know—you'll

just feel.

And they won't
confuse you

and they won't
lead you on.

It's simple.

If they want you,
they'll do anything

in their power
to have you.

They'll want you
in their lives

because

they *need you,*

because

they want you
and you *always*

have to be
ready

for something
like that.

Never shut the door.

THE STRUGGLE

Find yourself
through the struggle,

test yourself.

Emphasize on your
weaknesses.

Work on your doubts—on
your fears.

Face them.

Get uncomfortable.

Put yourself
through your own

personal hell.

Learn
what you're bad at

and put
the time in

to master it.

You already know
what you're good at.

You already know
what you can do

but the trick is,
to know

what you can't do—what
you think

you can't do.

Harden your mind,
strengthen your heart

and figure out
the impossible.

Get your heart broken.
Fail sometimes.

Let your insecurities
get the best

of you.

This is how
you're going to know

what your made of—what
you're capable of.

Find yourself
through the struggle.

Within it.
Find your smile.

Your peace.
Your hope.

Your dreams.

Your passion
and what you love.

You know
and I know,

and everyone knows
that only through pain

you will find
love.

That only through tears
will you find

laughter.

That only through failure
will you find

success.

That only through darkness
you will find

light.

You know
and I know

and everyone knows.

That this is true,
that through rain

you seek out
shelter

and through
your own struggle

you will find
you.

Amen.

Go through it.
Embrace it.

You will find
life

when you least
expect it

most.

The truth
is yours.

ABOVE ANYTHING

You can't do
people wrong

and expect them
to do you right.

Karma is real.

What comes around
goes around.

So be kind.

Treat people
with respect,

get your shit
together.

outstanding phrase.

And always
spread love

and laughter
above anything else.

WAITING TO SPEND

You spend
your time preparing

for a future
that isn't certain.

Preparing
for something

that might
never happen.

We are taught
to wait

for the uncertain.

We are taught
to think

that if it does happen
then it was meant

to be.

How painful
it is

to wait.

To believe
in what happens

in your life
only happens

because it was fate.

That you had
no control

over it.

The agony of this.
The tear of this.

The misconception
of this.

*Your life
is your life.*

What manifests
is based off your thoughts,

your actions,
your choices…

with

or without
consequence

or coincidence.

With
or without

invitation.

*Your life
is your life.*

Whether it be
torn to bits

or trapped
in a paradise trembling.

*Your life
is your life.*

And you have everything
but you also

have nothing.

You spend your life
preparing for a life

that isn't

—

even yours.

For a moment,
an event

that might *not* happen.

Don't wait for it.

Make it yours
without hesitation.

Without a proper plan.

Without following others.

Without a path
to guide you.

Do not wait,
make it yours,

all yours
but *really* make it

yours.

Really chase it,
even if you lose it—even

if you lose

everything.

Even if you gain
it all.

You spend your time
preparing

for a future
that isn't certain.

Preparing.
Practicing.
Waiting.

Living...
for a life

that could be yours
or not.

Do not wait.
Do not prepare.

Just go for it goddamnit!

Because your heart
is telling you

yes.

Because your mind
is telling you

no.

Because the ones
who love you

sometimes don't agree
with you

and the fake friends

you think
love you

don't really
give a *damn* about you.

Don't really
believe in you

but you have
a chance

to prove them wrong.

To prove yourself
EVERYTHING.

Go for it,

go all the way.

And don't spend your time
preparing

for a future
that isn't certain.

Spend it
on a future

that counts.

For a future
you know

that'll benefit you.

Spend it
on anything

but for Christ sakes,
do not spend

anything
on something

that's uncertain.

That's suicide.

Both spiritual
and mental.

*Your life
is your life.*

Make it count.
Make it beautiful.
Make it yours.

Amen.

INSPIRE ME

I admire you
because you don't let

the bullshit
stop you.

You don't let
the social commentaries

dictate
the way you feel.

You have this fire
in your eyes.

This deep passion
in your heart.

Never stop.
Never let go.

Keep going,
baby.

You inspire me.

From me to me
Love it.
enjoy it.

FRICTION, MAN

You need
a little friction

sometimes
with your lover,

a little chaos.

Because
you can't let things

become
too perfect.

If they do
then they become

dull
and boring.

And no one wants
that kind

of love.

And you shouldn't hope
for perfection

either
but you should hope
for just enough

to get you going.

Just enough
to keep you in love—enough

to stimulate
your senses...

to have you coming back
for more.

Wanting to give it
another shot

if it fails—making
it work

even if you know
you're doomed

from the very start.

And it works like this:

the more you give
the least you get

and vice versa.

Because sometimes
you'll get

the lower end
of the stick,

while other times
you won't.

A lover
can do that to you

and you give
so much power

to a lover
without even noticing it.

Without even
knowing what you've done

from the very start.

But don't
get it twisted.

Don't get it
confused.

It works both ways.

They destroy,
you rebuild.

They laugh,
you cry.

And sometimes
it'll happen to them

and sometimes
it'll happen

to you.

The balance is perfect.

The hurting
and the loving

is mutual.

Engrave this in
your mind,

in your heart
and in your soul.

You need
a little chaos

sometimes.

You need
a little disorder.

A little disagreement.

This I say
to those

who tell me
they cannot find love.

This I say
to the ones

who tell me
their hearts are broken.

To the givers.
To the romantics.

To those who feel
like they've lost

everything
and to the ones

who want
to believe.

Find a lover
who pushes you

toward the edge
but also

has the strength
to pull you

far from it.

Find a lover
who isn't afraid

to hurt you,
who isn't afraid

to heal you.

Find a lover
who tells you

when you're wrong,
who praises you

when you're right.

Who lights your fire,
who feeds it

and who gives it

the space it needs
when it needs

to breathe.

Find this
uncommon love

amongst the common lover
and give in to it.

Vow to it,
surrender to it...

through the good
and bad times.

The key is not to find
someone

who completes you
but to find

someone
who understands.

Someone
who is just as mad

as you
or just as passionate.

Find this person.

Love them.
Break them.

Hold them.
Save them.

And then,
do it

all over
again.

Do it

without thinking
twice.

I DON'T DESERVE THIS

It's sad
because sometimes

I feel
like I haven't

been loved
as hard

as I've loved.

Like I haven't
been cared for

as much
as I've cared.

It's hard for me
to come to this

realization.

Maybe I've spent
most of my time

chasing the wrong people—loving
the wrong people.
It hurts,

well
of course it does,

because my entire life
has been

dedicated
to people

I know
I don't deserve.

SOON ENOUGH

Be careful
with your health.

Stay focused.

Be patient
with yourself

and pay attention
to the way

people treat you.

Soon enough,
you'll know

who you deserve.

Time reveals
and heals.

Sometimes
time

is the only
friend you need

on your side.

TOO CLOSE

It seems
that almost everyone

you come across
is trying

to control
your love

because

they can't seem
to control

their own goddamn
lives.

They can't seem
to control

what to feel
or how to feel—when

to feel,
so they think

they have the right
to dictate

what you *should*
be feeling.

These are the wolves
amongst us.

The true devourers
of worlds.

They make you feel small.

They make you feel
as if

what you're doing
is wrong.

As if
the way you love

isn't
the right way.

These are the ones
who have yet

to love
themselves.

Who have yet
to know

what it is like
to go through

the fire.

Stay away
from these people

and never practice
what they commit—what

they preach.

Never fall into
what they believe in.

Never feed into
what they say

about you
or how they make you

and others
feel.

*They're wrong,
dead wrong.*

You're not weak.
You're not broken.

You're not lost
or confused.

Don't give in
to what they say.

They know nothing
about you.

Nothing
about real people,

about real
experience

and about real
love.

It's sad to say,
but it is true,

these people
who hurt you

don't know any better.

They barely understand
what they've done.

They barely understand
the consequence

of things.

The cause
and effect,

you know?

And then they wonder
why good people

like you
leave.

They wonder
why they feel alone.

Why they can't seem
to find someone

to stick around.

The questions bloom
and truthfully,

you won't be around
to answer them.

You'll be
somewhere else,

in another place,

in another moment,
in another world...

with someone
better.

With someone
who cares.

And you won't waste
a second thinking

of them
because

they never had
the guts

to love you
or to show you

how much
they cared.

All they did
was try to control you…

without knowing
how much

you needed

to spread
your wings.

You're a bird
and you need the sky

but you also
need someone

who'll teach you
how to fly.

The wind
is waiting.

YOU AND I

We're lovers
you and I.

We just want to
support,

encourage,
inspire,
help

and move the people
we love

but we get
taken for granted.

We feel
unappreciated

and maybe,

it is because

the amount of love
we give.

NOTHING AT ALL

I want you
to be a blessing

not a lesson.

Therefore,
I shouldn't have to

tell you
how to love me.

Do what your heart
tells you

then follow it
because you feel it.

Love me
with your soul

or nothing
at all.

A LITTLE RAIN

Pay attention
to the people

who have
their best interest

in you.

They care
more about you

and your feelings
than they do

about themselves.

Be real
with them.

Keep them
and show them

the sun
when they begin

to feel
a little rain.

DO THAT TO YOU

I'm different,
of course I am.

I've grown.
I've healed.

I've learned
and I've changed.

Time
and experience

and people
and love

will do that
to you.

WHAT FUELS YOU

Find what fuels you.

Find where
your inspiration dwells.

Live there.
Grow there.

Love there.
Breathe there.

You don't need
to prove your worth.

You don't need
to impress anyone.

You can be
anyone there,

even yourself.

Find
what moves you.

What gives you
the fire

to keep going
and never stop

searching

even if
it kills you.

It is
a beautiful thing

to chase
the things that make you

feel free.

Chase dreams not people.

OVER THINKING

At some point,
you have to stop

overthinking
about the people

who hurt you
and start

paying attention
to those

who are willing
to go through hell

and back
with you.

My lovely family
and friends.

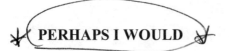

PERHAPS I WOULD

Yes
it is true.

There are nights
when I am

sad.

Nights
when I am

angry.

Nights
when I want

to be left
alone.

No one seems
to understand this.

No one seems
to catch on.

Everyone keeps asking
me

the wrong questions.

"Are you okay?"
"Do you feel better?"
"What's wrong?"

All these questions
but no one

is listening.

No one
is understanding

what it is
I feel.

It is true,
some nights

I desire someone
to be here with me.

Someone
to not talk to.

Someone
to sit with—lay

with quietly.

Someone
who'll stop asking me

these ridiculous
questions.

It is true,
I have a lot of friends

that care
but sometimes

I feel
like none of them

really know me.

Like none of them
could sit down

and tell me
who I am

or what
I should be doing.

Some nights,
I swear,

my heart becomes

a violent place—a
holy place.

Where war lingers.

Where conflict
is continuous.

Where the sounds
of the people

I used to be
keep me up

at night.

I want to be this.
I want to do that.

I want to love this.
I want to love that.

I want to move here
and then

a few weeks later,
I want to go

somewhere else.

I don't know

what to do.

I don't know
who I am

and I don't know
why.

It is true,
perhaps,

they are all
asking

the wrong things
but also
perhaps,

I wouldn't know
how to answer them

if they did.

Some nights,
I swear...

I feel as if
I am nothing

without you.

I am lost
and dim,

and sadly,

some nights
this hits me harder,

while other nights
it brings me back

from my

doom.

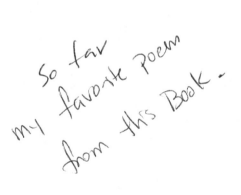

So far
my favorite poem
from this Book -

YOUR HEART

If they
love you

they'll be patient
with you.

They'll wait
for you

and try
to make sense

of the chaos
in your heart.

THE OTHER NIGHT

The other night
I thought

I had
a missed call

from you.

I was too busy
to grab the phone.

The other night
I thought

I read a text message
from you.

It said,

"Be kind to yourself.
Be gentle with yourself.

Consider your feelings
and why you feel

the way
you feel."

I looked twice
at the message

and it was from
my best friend.

The other night
I thought

I heard your voice—whispering
from the hallway...

mentioning
my name

but I was too
distracted

to make of it
but I am almost sure

it was you.

The other night
your favorite song

played on the radio.

It took to me
to the time

when we were young
and in love.

To the time
when you were still

here.

I quickly realized
the truth,

and how you've been gone
for the past

seven months.

The other night
I read

your last letter
you ever wrote to me...

and the last sentence
said:

"I'll never forget you."

And to this day
I hope

that is something

you meant—a
promise you're still

keeping.

The other night
I asked myself

why

I still held on.

Why
I still thought

of you
after all this time.

And out of nowhere
my sister texted me.

"Because I still
believe in you."

And exactly
two minutes later

she text me back
and said,

"Sorry that message was meant for my
husband."

And I sat there
and wondered why.

Why can't it all
be so simple.

Why couldn't loving you
last a little longer

and why
does holding on

feel like
open heart surgery...

connecting the fragments
within me

just to keep me
alive.

*I STILL FEEL YOU
IN MY HEART.*

I really connect with his
word cause of what Im going
through.

MY BROTHER

My heart
still belongs

to all
who've destroyed me.

To all
who've told me

they loved me
and to all

whom I thought
would always

be here.

It cannot be,
I know

but the heart
is weaker

than the mind.

The heart
is moved by this

charming idea,
by this dream,

that one day,
I would be able to wake up

and share
a cup a coffee with you.

That one day

the words that flow

out of your mouth
will crack the walls

and heal
your mother's heart.

The gravity is
heavy here.

The clouds are low
and the air

is pulled
from my lungs.

I think of you,
my sweet brother.

I think
of the last time

I saw you alive
and the last night

I said good-bye.

I miss you, man
and sometimes

I ache brilliantly,
swiftly,

and beautifully.

And sometimes
I write about you

to ease it all.

While other times,
I lose myself

in our childhood.

It was easier
back then,

that I can admit.

Among our friends
outside in the rain.

It almost feels
like a dream now.

It almost feels
like our memories

aren't real.

Like a dream
I've been to before.

You've been gone
too long,

my friend.

And some of us
still think of you

while some of us don't

but not me.

I've built
a tower just to reach you.

A tower
with all my hopes

and dreams
to keep you company.

Until all the people
you once loved

reunite
with you.

Until all the people
you need

are there.

And I hope
they reach you

in time.

I hope
none of them

arrive too late.

A WAY OUT

We search for people
in hopes

that maybe
someone out there

in the vastness
of the world

will feel
the brokenness

the loneliness
and the longing

to be held

the same way
that we do.

THE REST OF MY LIFE

I'm always thinking
about how my actions

and words
will affect people.

Both strangers
and those I love.

I try
to be careful

with my words.

I try
to use my voice

delicately
and precisely.

I don't what
to over indulge

people
and I definitely

don't want
to exhaust them

either.

I have a lot
to say.

A lot to do.

A lot to feel
and still,

a lot of growing up
to go through.

I don't want
to give people

the wrong impression
of me.

Although,
it is said

not to care
about what others

say or think
or feel

about you.

But I think

it's wrong,
in some sense,

because *I care.*

And maybe
I'm too naive

or too silly
or too immature

to think otherwise.

I care,

and maybe it's foolish
of me

to do so.

But I care
about other people.

I care
about how they perceive

me.

How they
preview my thoughts
and feelings.

How they
digest them

and if they understood me
the way I'd

want them to.

I don't want
to be confusing.

I don't want
to be unclear.

I want to say
what's in my heart.

I want to be
real.

And I want
to make sure

someone takes
something with them

once we depart...
on or off paper.

Maybe I care
far too much

then I should
but that's my flaw.

My curse.
My demon.

And that's why
it hurts

the way it hurts
and that's something

I have to
live with

for the rest of my life.

It is my
grand work

of art… to
leave something behind

that's capable
of doing

so much more.

MOVE ON PLEASE

Not everyone
you lose

is a loss.

The same people
who break you,

will be the ones
who make you.

They'll be the ones
who'll teach you

how to love.

How to forgive
and above all,

how to move on.

And those are very
important

lessons to learn in order,
to move on.

"THE SCIENCE OF…" SERIES
IS COMING SOON - SPRING OF 2020